GOALS JOURNAL

100 GOALS

by **Sandra Graves**

GOALS JOURNAL 100 GOALS

By Sandra Graves
Fitmaker Media

ISBN 978-0-9837242-8-5 (paperback)

Published by Rory Media   Printed in the United States of America

Write It Down. Believe. Make It Real.

GOAL 6

☐

☐

☐

☐

☐

NOTES

GOAL 7

Today's Date: ⬚⬚⬚⬚   **Target Date:** ⬚⬚⬚⬚

Date Completed: ⬚⬚⬚⬚   **Goal Accomplished:** ☐

GOAL (describe your ultimate goal and then break it down under mini goals)

GOAL TYPE

- ◯ Personal
- ◯ Health & Fitness
- ◯ Relationships
- ◯ Financial
- ◯ Career
- ◯ Travel
- ◯ Lifetime
- ◯ Other

MINI GOALS (include up to 10 steps to achieve main goal)

☐

☐

☐

☐

☐

GOAL 7

☐

☐

☐

☐

☐

NOTES

GOAL 8

Today's Date: **Target Date:**

Date Completed: **Goal Accomplished:** ☐

GOAL   (describe your ultimate goal and then break it down under mini goals)

GOAL TYPE

- ◯ Personal
- ◯ Health & Fitness
- ◯ Relationships
- ◯ Financial
- ◯ Career
- ◯ Travel
- ◯ Lifetime
- ◯ Other

MINI GOALS   (include up to 10 steps to achieve main goal)

☐

☐

☐

☐

☐

GOAL 8

- [ ]
- [ ]
- [ ]
- [ ]
- [ ]

NOTES

GOAL 9

Today's Date: **Target Date:**

Date Completed: **Goal Accomplished:** ☐

GOAL (describe your ultimate goal and then break it down under mini goals)

GOAL TYPE

- ○ Personal
- ○ Health & Fitness
- ○ Relationships
- ○ Financial
- ○ Career
- ○ Travel
- ○ Lifetime
- ○ Other

MINI GOALS (include up to 10 steps to achieve main goal)

☐

☐

☐

☐

☐

GOAL 9

☐

☐

☐

☐

☐

GOAL 10

Today's Date: **Target Date:**

Date Completed: **Goal Accomplished:** ☐

GOAL (describe your ultimate goal and then break it down under mini goals)

GOAL TYPE

- ○ Personal
- ○ Health & Fitness
- ○ Relationships
- ○ Financial
- ○ Career
- ○ Travel
- ○ Lifetime
- ○ Other

MINI GOALS (include up to 10 steps to achieve main goal)

☐

☐

☐

☐

☐

GOAL 10

☐

☐

☐

☐

☐

NOTES

GOAL 11

Today's Date: **Target Date:**

Date Completed: **Goal Accomplished:** ☐

GOAL (describe your ultimate goal and then break it down under mini goals)

GOAL TYPE

○ Personal   ○ Health & Fitness   ○ Relationships

○ Financial   ○ Career   ○ Travel   ○ Lifetime

○ Other

MINI GOALS (include up to 10 steps to achieve main goal)

☐

☐

☐

☐

☐

GOAL 11

☐

☐

☐

☐

☐

NOTES

GOAL 12

Today's Date: **Target Date:**

Date Completed: **Goal Accomplished:** ☐

GOAL (describe your ultimate goal and then break it down under mini goals)

GOAL TYPE

○ Personal   ○ Health & Fitness   ○ Relationships

○ Financial   ○ Career   ○ Travel   ○ Lifetime

○ Other

MINI GOALS (include up to 10 steps to achieve main goal)

☐

☐

☐

☐

☐

GOAL 12

☐

☐

☐

☐

☐

NOTES

GOAL 13

Today's Date: **Target Date:**

Date Completed: **Goal Accomplished:** ☐

GOAL (describe your ultimate goal and then break it down under mini goals)

GOAL TYPE

- ○ Personal   ○ Health & Fitness   ○ Relationships
- ○ Financial   ○ Career   ○ Travel   ○ Lifetime
- ○ Other

MINI GOALS (include up to 10 steps to achieve main goal)

- ☐
- ☐
- ☐
- ☐
- ☐

GOAL 13

☐

☐

☐

☐

☐

NOTES

GOAL 14

Today's Date: **Target Date:**

Date Completed: **Goal Accomplished:** ☐

GOAL (describe your ultimate goal and then break it down under mini goals)

GOAL TYPE

○ Personal   ○ Health & Fitness   ○ Relationships

○ Financial   ○ Career   ○ Travel   ○ Lifetime

○ Other

MINI GOALS (include up to 10 steps to achieve main goal)

☐

☐

☐

☐

☐

GOAL 14

☐

☐

☐

☐

☐

NOTES

GOAL 15

Today's Date: ⬚⬚⬚⬚⬚   **Target Date:** ⬚⬚⬚⬚⬚

Date Completed: ⬚⬚⬚⬚⬚   **Goal Accomplished:** ☐

GOAL (describe your ultimate goal and then break it down under mini goals)

GOAL TYPE

○ Personal   ○ Health & Fitness   ○ Relationships

○ Financial   ○ Career   ○ Travel   ○ Lifetime

○ Other

MINI GOALS (include up to 10 steps to achieve main goal)

☐

☐

☐

☐

☐

GOAL 15

☐

☐

☐

☐

☐

NOTES

GOAL 16

Today's Date: 　　　　　　**Target Date:**

Date Completed: 　　　　　　**Goal Accomplished:** ☐

GOAL (describe your ultimate goal and then break it down under mini goals)

GOAL TYPE

○ Personal　　　○ Health & Fitness　　　○ Relationships

○ Financial　　　○ Career　　　○ Travel　　　○ Lifetime

○ Other

MINI GOALS (include up to 10 steps to achieve main goal)

☐

☐

☐

☐

☐

GOAL 16

☐

☐

☐

☐

☐

NOTES

GOAL 17

Today's Date: **Target Date:**

Date Completed: **Goal Accomplished:** ☐

GOAL (describe your ultimate goal and then break it down under mini goals)

GOAL TYPE

○ Personal   ○ Health & Fitness   ○ Relationships

○ Financial   ○ Career   ○ Travel   ○ Lifetime

○ Other

MINI GOALS (include up to 10 steps to achieve main goal)

☐

☐

☐

☐

☐

GOAL 17

☐

☐

☐

☐

☐

NOTES

GOAL 18

Today's Date: ⬚⬚⬚⬚⬚   **Target Date:** ⬚⬚⬚⬚⬚

Date Completed: ⬚⬚⬚⬚⬚   **Goal Accomplished:** ☐

GOAL   (describe your ultimate goal and then break it down under mini goals)

GOAL TYPE

○ Personal   ○ Health & Fitness   ○ Relationships

○ Financial   ○ Career   ○ Travel   ○ Lifetime

○ Other

MINI GOALS   (include up to 10 steps to achieve main goal)

☐

☐

☐

☐

☐

GOAL 18

☐

☐

☐

☐

☐

NOTES

GOAL 19

Today's Date: ⬚⬚⬚⬚⬚   **Target Date:** ⬚⬚⬚⬚⬚

Date Completed: ⬚⬚⬚⬚⬚   **Goal Accomplished:** ☐

GOAL	(describe your ultimate goal and then break it down under mini goals)

GOAL TYPE	○ Personal	○ Health & Fitness	○ Relationships
○ Financial	○ Career	○ Travel	○ Lifetime
○ Other			

MINI GOALS (include up to 10 steps to achieve main goal)

☐

☐

☐

☐

☐

GOAL 19

- [ ]
- [ ]
- [ ]
- [ ]
- [ ]

NOTES

GOAL 20

Today's Date: **Target Date:**

Date Completed: **Goal Accomplished:** ☐

GOAL (describe your ultimate goal and then break it down under mini goals)

GOAL TYPE

- ○ Personal
- ○ Health & Fitness
- ○ Relationships
- ○ Financial
- ○ Career
- ○ Travel
- ○ Lifetime
- ○ Other

MINI GOALS (include up to 10 steps to achieve main goal)

☐

☐

☐

☐

☐

GOAL 20

☐

☐

☐

☐

☐

NOTES

GOAL 21

Today's Date: _____   **Target Date:** _____

Date Completed: _____   **Goal Accomplished:** ☐

GOAL (describe your ultimate goal and then break it down under mini goals)

GOAL TYPE
○ Personal   ○ Health & Fitness   ○ Relationships
○ Financial   ○ Career   ○ Travel   ○ Lifetime
○ Other

MINI GOALS (include up to 10 steps to achieve main goal)

☐

☐

☐

☐

☐

GOAL 21

- [ ]
- [ ]
- [ ]
- [ ]
- [ ]

NOTES

GOAL 22

Today's Date: **Target Date:**

Date Completed: **Goal Accomplished:** ☐

GOAL (describe your ultimate goal and then break it down under mini goals)

GOAL TYPE

- ◯ Personal
- ◯ Health & Fitness
- ◯ Relationships
- ◯ Financial
- ◯ Career
- ◯ Travel
- ◯ Lifetime
- ◯ Other

MINI GOALS (include up to 10 steps to achieve main goal)

- ☐
- ☐
- ☐
- ☐
- ☐

GOAL 22

☐

☐

☐

☐

☐

NOTES

GOAL 23

Today's Date: **Target Date:**

Date Completed: **Goal Accomplished:** ☐

GOAL   (describe your ultimate goal and then break it down under mini goals)

GOAL TYPE

- ◯ Personal
- ◯ Health & Fitness
- ◯ Relationships
- ◯ Financial
- ◯ Career
- ◯ Travel
- ◯ Lifetime
- ◯ Other

MINI GOALS   (include up to 10 steps to achieve main goal)

☐

☐

☐

☐

☐

GOAL 23

☐

☐

☐

☐

☐

NOTES

GOAL 24

Today's Date: _____   **Target Date:** _____

Date Completed: _____   **Goal Accomplished:** ☐

GOAL	(describe your ultimate goal and then break it down under mini goals)

GOAL TYPE	○ Personal	○ Health & Fitness	○ Relationships
○ Financial	○ Career	○ Travel	○ Lifetime
○ Other			

MINI GOALS (include up to 10 steps to achieve main goal)

☐

☐

☐

☐

☐

GOAL 24

☐

☐

☐

☐

☐

GOAL 25

Today's Date: **Target Date:**

Date Completed: **Goal Accomplished:** ☐

GOAL (describe your ultimate goal and then break it down under mini goals)

GOAL TYPE

- ◯ Personal
- ◯ Health & Fitness
- ◯ Relationships
- ◯ Financial
- ◯ Career
- ◯ Travel
- ◯ Lifetime
- ◯ Other

MINI GOALS (include up to 10 steps to achieve main goal)

☐

☐

☐

☐

☐

GOAL 25

☐

☐

☐

☐

☐

GOAL 26

Today's Date: **Target Date:**

Date Completed: **Goal Accomplished:** ☐

GOAL (describe your ultimate goal and then break it down under mini goals)

GOAL TYPE

- ◯ Personal
- ◯ Health & Fitness
- ◯ Relationships
- ◯ Financial
- ◯ Career
- ◯ Travel
- ◯ Lifetime
- ◯ Other

MINI GOALS (include up to 10 steps to achieve main goal)

- ☐
- ☐
- ☐
- ☐
- ☐

GOAL 26

☐

☐

☐

☐

☐

NOTES

GOAL 27

Today's Date: **Target Date:**

Date Completed: **Goal Accomplished:** ☐

GOAL (describe your ultimate goal and then break it down under mini goals)

GOAL TYPE
- ○ Personal
- ○ Health & Fitness
- ○ Relationships
- ○ Financial
- ○ Career
- ○ Travel
- ○ Lifetime
- ○ Other

MINI GOALS (include up to 10 steps to achieve main goal)

☐

☐

☐

☐

☐

GOAL 27

☐

☐

☐

☐

☐

GOAL 28

Today's Date: **Target Date:**

Date Completed: **Goal Accomplished:** ☐

GOAL (describe your ultimate goal and then break it down under mini goals)

GOAL TYPE

- ○ Personal
- ○ Health & Fitness
- ○ Relationships
- ○ Financial
- ○ Career
- ○ Travel
- ○ Lifetime
- ○ Other

MINI GOALS (include up to 10 steps to achieve main goal)

☐

☐

☐

☐

☐

GOAL 28

- [ ]
- [ ]
- [ ]
- [ ]
- [ ]

NOTES

GOAL 29

Today's Date: _____   **Target Date:** _____

Date Completed: _____   **Goal Accomplished:** ☐

GOAL	(describe your ultimate goal and then break it down under mini goals)

GOAL TYPE	○ Personal	○ Health & Fitness	○ Relationships
○ Financial	○ Career	○ Travel	○ Lifetime
○ Other			

MINI GOALS	(include up to 10 steps to achieve main goal)

☐

☐

☐

☐

☐

GOAL 29

☐

☐

☐

☐

☐

NOTES

GOAL 30

Today's Date: _____   **Target Date:** _____

Date Completed: _____   **Goal Accomplished:** ☐

GOAL	(describe your ultimate goal and then break it down under mini goals)

GOAL TYPE	○ Personal	○ Health & Fitness	○ Relationships
○ Financial	○ Career	○ Travel	○ Lifetime
○ Other			

MINI GOALS (include up to 10 steps to achieve main goal)

☐

☐

☐

☐

☐

GOAL 30

☐

☐

☐

☐

☐

NOTES

GOAL 31

Today's Date: **Target Date:**

Date Completed: **Goal Accomplished:** ☐

GOAL (describe your ultimate goal and then break it down under mini goals)

GOAL TYPE

- ○ Personal
- ○ Health & Fitness
- ○ Relationships
- ○ Financial
- ○ Career
- ○ Travel
- ○ Lifetime
- ○ Other

MINI GOALS (include up to 10 steps to achieve main goal)

- ☐
- ☐
- ☐
- ☐
- ☐

GOAL 31

☐

☐

☐

☐

☐

NOTES

GOAL 32

Today's Date: **Target Date:**

Date Completed: **Goal Accomplished:** ☐

GOAL (describe your ultimate goal and then break it down under mini goals)

GOAL TYPE

○ Personal   ○ Health & Fitness   ○ Relationships

○ Financial   ○ Career   ○ Travel   ○ Lifetime

○ Other

MINI GOALS (include up to 10 steps to achieve main goal)

☐

☐

☐

☐

☐

GOAL 32

☐

☐

☐

☐

☐

NOTES

GOAL 33

Today's Date: **Target Date:**

Date Completed: **Goal Accomplished:** ☐

GOAL (describe your ultimate goal and then break it down under mini goals)

GOAL TYPE

◯ Personal   ◯ Health & Fitness   ◯ Relationships

◯ Financial   ◯ Career   ◯ Travel   ◯ Lifetime

◯ Other

MINI GOALS (include up to 10 steps to achieve main goal)

☐

☐

☐

☐

☐

GOAL 33

☐

☐

☐

☐

☐

NOTES

GOAL 34

Today's Date: **Target Date:**

Date Completed: **Goal Accomplished:** ☐

GOAL (describe your ultimate goal and then break it down under mini goals)

GOAL TYPE

○ Personal   ○ Health & Fitness   ○ Relationships

○ Financial   ○ Career   ○ Travel   ○ Lifetime

○ Other

MINI GOALS (include up to 10 steps to achieve main goal)

☐

☐

☐

☐

☐

GOAL 34

☐

☐

☐

☐

☐

GOAL 35

Today's Date: **Target Date:**

Date Completed: **Goal Accomplished:** ☐

GOAL (describe your ultimate goal and then break it down under mini goals)

GOAL TYPE

○ Personal   ○ Health & Fitness   ○ Relationships

○ Financial   ○ Career   ○ Travel   ○ Lifetime

○ Other

MINI GOALS (include up to 10 steps to achieve main goal)

☐

☐

☐

☐

☐

GOAL 35

☐

☐

☐

☐

☐

NOTES

GOAL 36

Today's Date: _____   **Target Date:** _____

Date Completed: _____   **Goal Accomplished:** ☐

GOAL (describe your ultimate goal and then break it down under mini goals)

GOAL TYPE

○ Personal   ○ Health & Fitness   ○ Relationships

○ Financial   ○ Career   ○ Travel   ○ Lifetime

○ Other

MINI GOALS (include up to 10 steps to achieve main goal)

☐

☐

☐

☐

☐

GOAL 36

☐

☐

☐

☐

☐

GOAL 37

Today's Date: **Target Date:**

Date Completed: **Goal Accomplished:** ☐

GOAL (describe your ultimate goal and then break it down under mini goals)

GOAL TYPE

- ◯ Personal
- ◯ Health & Fitness
- ◯ Relationships
- ◯ Financial
- ◯ Career
- ◯ Travel
- ◯ Lifetime
- ◯ Other

MINI GOALS (include up to 10 steps to achieve main goal)

- ☐
- ☐
- ☐
- ☐
- ☐

GOAL 37

☐

☐

☐

☐

☐

GOAL 38

Today's Date: ⬚   **Target Date:** ⬚

Date Completed: ⬚   **Goal Accomplished:** ☐

GOAL (describe your ultimate goal and then break it down under mini goals)

GOAL TYPE

○ Personal   ○ Health & Fitness   ○ Relationships

○ Financial   ○ Career   ○ Travel   ○ Lifetime

○ Other

MINI GOALS (include up to 10 steps to achieve main goal)

☐

☐

☐

☐

☐

GOAL 38

☐

☐

☐

☐

☐

NOTES

GOAL 39

Today's Date: **Target Date:**

Date Completed: **Goal Accomplished:** ☐

GOAL   (describe your ultimate goal and then break it down under mini goals)

GOAL TYPE

- ◯ Personal
- ◯ Health & Fitness
- ◯ Relationships
- ◯ Financial
- ◯ Career
- ◯ Travel
- ◯ Lifetime
- ◯ Other

MINI GOALS   (include up to 10 steps to achieve main goal)

☐

☐

☐

☐

☐

GOAL 39

☐

☐

☐

☐

☐

NOTES

GOAL 40

Today's Date: _____   **Target Date:** _____

Date Completed: _____   **Goal Accomplished:** ☐

GOAL (describe your ultimate goal and then break it down under mini goals)

GOAL TYPE
- ○ Personal
- ○ Health & Fitness
- ○ Relationships
- ○ Financial
- ○ Career
- ○ Travel
- ○ Lifetime
- ○ Other

MINI GOALS (include up to 10 steps to achieve main goal)

☐

☐

☐

☐

☐

GOAL 40

☐

☐

☐

☐

☐

GOAL 41

Today's Date: **Target Date:**

Date Completed: **Goal Accomplished:** ☐

GOAL (describe your ultimate goal and then break it down under mini goals)

GOAL TYPE

○ Personal   ○ Health & Fitness   ○ Relationships

○ Financial   ○ Career   ○ Travel   ○ Lifetime

○ Other

MINI GOALS (include up to 10 steps to achieve main goal)

☐

☐

☐

☐

☐

GOAL 41

☐

☐

☐

☐

☐

NOTES

GOAL 42

Today's Date: _____   **Target Date:** _____

Date Completed: _____   **Goal Accomplished:** ☐

GOAL	(describe your ultimate goal and then break it down under mini goals)

GOAL TYPE	○ Personal	○ Health & Fitness	○ Relationships
○ Financial	○ Career	○ Travel	○ Lifetime
○ Other			

MINI GOALS (include up to 10 steps to achieve main goal)

☐

☐

☐

☐

☐

GOAL 42

☐

☐

☐

☐

☐

NOTES

GOAL 43

Today's Date: **Target Date:**

Date Completed: **Goal Accomplished:** ☐

GOAL (describe your ultimate goal and then break it down under mini goals)

GOAL TYPE

- ◯ Personal
- ◯ Health & Fitness
- ◯ Relationships
- ◯ Financial
- ◯ Career
- ◯ Travel
- ◯ Lifetime
- ◯ Other

MINI GOALS (include up to 10 steps to achieve main goal)

- ☐
- ☐
- ☐
- ☐
- ☐

GOAL 43

☐

☐

☐

☐

☐

NOTES

GOAL 44

Today's Date: **Target Date:**

Date Completed: **Goal Accomplished:** ☐

GOAL (describe your ultimate goal and then break it down under mini goals)

GOAL TYPE
- ○ Personal
- ○ Health & Fitness
- ○ Relationships
- ○ Financial
- ○ Career
- ○ Travel
- ○ Lifetime
- ○ Other

MINI GOALS (include up to 10 steps to achieve main goal)

☐

☐

☐

☐

☐

GOAL 44

☐

☐

☐

☐

☐

GOAL 45

Today's Date: **Target Date:**

Date Completed: **Goal Accomplished:** ☐

GOAL   (describe your ultimate goal and then break it down under mini goals)

GOAL TYPE

- ◯ Personal
- ◯ Health & Fitness
- ◯ Relationships
- ◯ Financial
- ◯ Career
- ◯ Travel
- ◯ Lifetime
- ◯ Other

MINI GOALS   (include up to 10 steps to achieve main goal)

☐

☐

☐

☐

☐

GOAL 45

☐

☐

☐

☐

☐

GOAL 46

Today's Date: _____ **Target Date:** _____

Date Completed: _____ **Goal Accomplished:** ☐

GOAL (describe your ultimate goal and then break it down under mini goals)

GOAL TYPE

- ○ Personal
- ○ Health & Fitness
- ○ Relationships
- ○ Financial
- ○ Career
- ○ Travel
- ○ Lifetime
- ○ Other

MINI GOALS (include up to 10 steps to achieve main goal)

☐

☐

☐

☐

☐

GOAL 46

☐

☐

☐

☐

☐

GOAL 47

Today's Date: **Target Date:**

Date Completed: **Goal Accomplished:** ☐

GOAL   (describe your ultimate goal and then break it down under mini goals)

GOAL TYPE

- ◯ Personal
- ◯ Health & Fitness
- ◯ Relationships
- ◯ Financial
- ◯ Career
- ◯ Travel
- ◯ Lifetime
- ◯ Other

MINI GOALS   (include up to 10 steps to achieve main goal)

☐

☐

☐

☐

☐

GOAL 47

☐

☐

☐

☐

☐

GOAL 48

Today's Date: **Target Date:**

Date Completed: **Goal Accomplished:** ☐

GOAL (describe your ultimate goal and then break it down under mini goals)

GOAL TYPE

- ◯ Personal
- ◯ Health & Fitness
- ◯ Relationships
- ◯ Financial
- ◯ Career
- ◯ Travel
- ◯ Lifetime
- ◯ Other

MINI GOALS (include up to 10 steps to achieve main goal)

- ☐
- ☐
- ☐
- ☐
- ☐

GOAL 48

- [ ]
- [ ]
- [ ]
- [ ]
- [ ]

NOTES

GOAL 49

Today's Date: **Target Date:**

Date Completed: **Goal Accomplished:** ☐

GOAL (describe your ultimate goal and then break it down under mini goals)

GOAL TYPE

- ○ Personal
- ○ Health & Fitness
- ○ Relationships
- ○ Financial
- ○ Career
- ○ Travel
- ○ Lifetime
- ○ Other

MINI GOALS (include up to 10 steps to achieve main goal)

☐

☐

☐

☐

☐

GOAL 49

☐

☐

☐

☐

☐

NOTES

GOAL 50

Today's Date: **Target Date:**

Date Completed: **Goal Accomplished:** ☐

GOAL (describe your ultimate goal and then break it down under mini goals)

GOAL TYPE

- ○ Personal
- ○ Health & Fitness
- ○ Relationships
- ○ Financial
- ○ Career
- ○ Travel
- ○ Lifetime
- ○ Other

MINI GOALS (include up to 10 steps to achieve main goal)

☐

☐

☐

☐

☐

GOAL 50

☐

☐

☐

☐

☐

NOTES

GOAL 51

Today's Date: **Target Date:**

Date Completed: **Goal Accomplished:** ☐

GOAL (describe your ultimate goal and then break it down under mini goals)

GOAL TYPE

- ○ Personal
- ○ Health & Fitness
- ○ Relationships
- ○ Financial
- ○ Career
- ○ Travel
- ○ Lifetime
- ○ Other

MINI GOALS (include up to 10 steps to achieve main goal)

☐

☐

☐

☐

☐

GOAL 51

☐

☐

☐

☐

☐

GOAL 52

Today's Date: **Target Date:**

Date Completed: **Goal Accomplished:** ☐

GOAL (describe your ultimate goal and then break it down under mini goals)

GOAL TYPE

◯ Personal   ◯ Health & Fitness   ◯ Relationships

◯ Financial   ◯ Career   ◯ Travel   ◯ Lifetime

◯ Other

MINI GOALS (include up to 10 steps to achieve main goal)

☐

☐

☐

☐

☐

GOAL 52

☐

☐

☐

☐

☐

NOTES

GOAL 53

Today's Date: _____   **Target Date:** _____

Date Completed: _____   **Goal Accomplished:** ☐

GOAL (describe your ultimate goal and then break it down under mini goals)

GOAL TYPE
- ○ Personal
- ○ Health & Fitness
- ○ Relationships
- ○ Financial
- ○ Career
- ○ Travel
- ○ Lifetime
- ○ Other

MINI GOALS (include up to 10 steps to achieve main goal)

- ☐
- ☐
- ☐
- ☐
- ☐

GOAL 53

☐

☐

☐

☐

☐

NOTES

GOAL 54

Today's Date: _____   **Target Date:** _____

Date Completed: _____   **Goal Accomplished:** ☐

GOAL	(describe your ultimate goal and then break it down under mini goals)

GOAL TYPE			
○ Personal	○ Health & Fitness	○ Relationships
○ Financial	○ Career	○ Travel	○ Lifetime
○ Other			

MINI GOALS (include up to 10 steps to achieve main goal)

☐

☐

☐

☐

☐

GOAL 54

☐

☐

☐

☐

☐

NOTES

GOAL 55

Today's Date: _____   **Target Date:** _____

Date Completed: _____   **Goal Accomplished:** ☐

GOAL (describe your ultimate goal and then break it down under mini goals)

GOAL TYPE

○ Personal   ○ Health & Fitness   ○ Relationships

○ Financial   ○ Career   ○ Travel   ○ Lifetime

○ Other

MINI GOALS (include up to 10 steps to achieve main goal)

☐

☐

☐

☐

☐

GOAL 55

☐

☐

☐

☐

☐

GOAL 56

Today's Date: **Target Date:**

Date Completed: **Goal Accomplished:** ☐

GOAL (describe your ultimate goal and then break it down under mini goals)

GOAL TYPE

- ○ Personal
- ○ Health & Fitness
- ○ Relationships
- ○ Financial
- ○ Career
- ○ Travel
- ○ Lifetime
- ○ Other

MINI GOALS (include up to 10 steps to achieve main goal)

- ☐
- ☐
- ☐
- ☐
- ☐

GOAL 56

☐

☐

☐

☐

☐

GOAL 57

Today's Date: **Target Date:**

Date Completed: **Goal Accomplished:** ☐

GOAL (describe your ultimate goal and then break it down under mini goals)

GOAL TYPE

○ Personal   ○ Health & Fitness   ○ Relationships

○ Financial   ○ Career   ○ Travel   ○ Lifetime

○ Other

MINI GOALS (include up to 10 steps to achieve main goal)

☐

☐

☐

☐

☐

GOAL 57

☐

☐

☐

☐

☐

GOAL 58

Today's Date: | **Target Date:**

Date Completed: | **Goal Accomplished:** ☐

GOAL (describe your ultimate goal and then break it down under mini goals)

GOAL TYPE

○ Personal ○ Health & Fitness ○ Relationships

○ Financial ○ Career ○ Travel ○ Lifetime

○ Other

MINI GOALS (include up to 10 steps to achieve main goal)

☐

☐

☐

☐

☐

GOAL 58

☐

☐

☐

☐

☐

NOTES

GOAL 59

Today's Date: _____   **Target Date:** _____

Date Completed: _____   **Goal Accomplished:** ☐

GOAL (describe your ultimate goal and then break it down under mini goals)

GOAL TYPE

- ○ Personal
- ○ Health & Fitness
- ○ Relationships
- ○ Financial
- ○ Career
- ○ Travel
- ○ Lifetime
- ○ Other

MINI GOALS (include up to 10 steps to achieve main goal)

☐

☐

☐

☐

☐

GOAL 59

- [ ]
- [ ]
- [ ]
- [ ]
- [ ]

NOTES

GOAL 60

Today's Date: **Target Date:**

Date Completed: **Goal Accomplished:** ☐

GOAL (describe your ultimate goal and then break it down under mini goals)

GOAL TYPE

- ○ Personal
- ○ Health & Fitness
- ○ Relationships
- ○ Financial
- ○ Career
- ○ Travel
- ○ Lifetime
- ○ Other

MINI GOALS (include up to 10 steps to achieve main goal)

- ☐
- ☐
- ☐
- ☐
- ☐

GOAL 60

- [ ]
- [ ]
- [ ]
- [ ]
- [ ]

NOTES

GOAL 61

Today's Date: **Target Date:**

Date Completed: **Goal Accomplished:** ☐

GOAL (describe your ultimate goal and then break it down under mini goals)

GOAL TYPE

◯ Personal   ◯ Health & Fitness   ◯ Relationships

◯ Financial   ◯ Career   ◯ Travel   ◯ Lifetime

◯ Other

MINI GOALS (include up to 10 steps to achieve main goal)

☐

☐

☐

☐

☐

GOAL 61

☐

☐

☐

☐

☐

NOTES

GOAL 62

Today's Date: **Target Date:**

Date Completed: **Goal Accomplished:** ☐

GOAL (describe your ultimate goal and then break it down under mini goals)

GOAL TYPE
○ Personal ○ Health & Fitness ○ Relationships
○ Financial ○ Career ○ Travel ○ Lifetime
○ Other

MINI GOALS (include up to 10 steps to achieve main goal)

☐

☐

☐

☐

☐

GOAL 62

☐

☐

☐

☐

☐

NOTES

GOAL 63

Today's Date: ⬚⬚⬚⬚⬚⬚⬚⬚   **Target Date:** ⬚⬚⬚⬚⬚⬚⬚⬚

Date Completed: ⬚⬚⬚⬚⬚⬚⬚⬚   **Goal Accomplished:** ☐

GOAL (describe your ultimate goal and then break it down under mini goals)

GOAL TYPE

○ Personal   ○ Health & Fitness   ○ Relationships

○ Financial   ○ Career   ○ Travel   ○ Lifetime

○ Other

MINI GOALS (include up to 10 steps to achieve main goal)

☐

☐

☐

☐

☐

GOAL 63

☐

☐

☐

☐

☐

NOTES

GOAL 64

Today's Date: **Target Date:**

Date Completed: **Goal Accomplished:** ☐

GOAL (describe your ultimate goal and then break it down under mini goals)

GOAL TYPE

- ◯ Personal
- ◯ Health & Fitness
- ◯ Relationships
- ◯ Financial
- ◯ Career
- ◯ Travel
- ◯ Lifetime
- ◯ Other

MINI GOALS (include up to 10 steps to achieve main goal)

- ☐
- ☐
- ☐
- ☐
- ☐

GOAL 64

☐

☐

☐

☐

☐

GOAL 65

Today's Date: **Target Date:**

Date Completed: **Goal Accomplished:** ☐

GOAL (describe your ultimate goal and then break it down under mini goals)

GOAL TYPE

- ○ Personal
- ○ Health & Fitness
- ○ Relationships
- ○ Financial
- ○ Career
- ○ Travel
- ○ Lifetime
- ○ Other

MINI GOALS (include up to 10 steps to achieve main goal)

☐

☐

☐

☐

☐

GOAL 65

☐
☐
☐
☐
☐

NOTES

GOAL 66

Today's Date: **Target Date:**

Date Completed: **Goal Accomplished:** ☐

GOAL   (describe your ultimate goal and then break it down under mini goals)

GOAL TYPE

○ Personal   ○ Health & Fitness   ○ Relationships

○ Financial   ○ Career   ○ Travel   ○ Lifetime

○ Other

MINI GOALS   (include up to 10 steps to achieve main goal)

☐

☐

☐

☐

☐

GOAL 66

☐

☐

☐

☐

☐

GOAL 67

Today's Date: ⬚⬚⬚⬚⬚⬚⬚ **Target Date:** ⬚⬚⬚⬚⬚⬚⬚

Date Completed: ⬚⬚⬚⬚⬚⬚⬚ **Goal Accomplished:** ☐

GOAL	(describe your ultimate goal and then break it down under mini goals)

GOAL TYPE			
○ Personal	○ Health & Fitness	○ Relationships	
○ Financial	○ Career	○ Travel	○ Lifetime
○ Other			

MINI GOALS (include up to 10 steps to achieve main goal)

☐

☐

☐

☐

☐

GOAL 67

☐

☐

☐

☐

☐

GOAL 68

Today's Date: **Target Date:**

Date Completed: **Goal Accomplished:** ☐

GOAL (describe your ultimate goal and then break it down under mini goals)

GOAL TYPE

- ◯ Personal
- ◯ Health & Fitness
- ◯ Relationships
- ◯ Financial
- ◯ Career
- ◯ Travel
- ◯ Lifetime
- ◯ Other

MINI GOALS (include up to 10 steps to achieve main goal)

☐

☐

☐

☐

☐

GOAL 68

☐

☐

☐

☐

☐

NOTES

GOAL 69

Today's Date: **Target Date:**

Date Completed: **Goal Accomplished:** ☐

GOAL (describe your ultimate goal and then break it down under mini goals)

GOAL TYPE

○ Personal   ○ Health & Fitness   ○ Relationships

○ Financial   ○ Career   ○ Travel   ○ Lifetime

○ Other

MINI GOALS (include up to 10 steps to achieve main goal)

☐

☐

☐

☐

☐

GOAL 69

☐

☐

☐

☐

☐

NOTES

GOAL 70

Today's Date: **Target Date:**

Date Completed: **Goal Accomplished:** ☐

GOAL (describe your ultimate goal and then break it down under mini goals)

GOAL TYPE
- ○ Personal
- ○ Health & Fitness
- ○ Relationships
- ○ Financial
- ○ Career
- ○ Travel
- ○ Lifetime
- ○ Other

MINI GOALS (include up to 10 steps to achieve main goal)

☐

☐

☐

☐

☐

GOAL 70

☐

☐

☐

☐

☐

NOTES

GOAL 71

Today's Date: ⬚⬚⬚⬚⬚⬚⬚⬚ **Target Date:** ⬚⬚⬚⬚⬚⬚⬚

Date Completed: ⬚⬚⬚⬚⬚⬚⬚ **Goal Accomplished:** ☐

GOAL (describe your ultimate goal and then break it down under mini goals)

GOAL TYPE

○ Personal ○ Health & Fitness ○ Relationships

○ Financial ○ Career ○ Travel ○ Lifetime

○ Other

MINI GOALS (include up to 10 steps to achieve main goal)

☐

☐

☐

☐

☐

GOAL 71

- [ ]
- [ ]
- [ ]
- [ ]
- [ ]

NOTES

GOAL 72

Today's Date: ‌   **Target Date:**

Date Completed: **Goal Accomplished:** ☐

GOAL (describe your ultimate goal and then break it down under mini goals)

GOAL TYPE

- ◯ Personal
- ◯ Health & Fitness
- ◯ Relationships
- ◯ Financial
- ◯ Career
- ◯ Travel
- ◯ Lifetime
- ◯ Other

MINI GOALS (include up to 10 steps to achieve main goal)

- ☐
- ☐
- ☐
- ☐
- ☐

GOAL 72

☐

☐

☐

☐

☐

GOAL 73

Today's Date: **Target Date:**

Date Completed: **Goal Accomplished:** ☐

GOAL (describe your ultimate goal and then break it down under mini goals)

GOAL TYPE

- ○ Personal
- ○ Health & Fitness
- ○ Relationships
- ○ Financial
- ○ Career
- ○ Travel
- ○ Lifetime
- ○ Other

MINI GOALS (include up to 10 steps to achieve main goal)

☐

☐

☐

☐

☐

GOAL 73

☐

☐

☐

☐

☐

GOAL 74

Today's Date: **Target Date:**

Date Completed: **Goal Accomplished:** ☐

GOAL   (describe your ultimate goal and then break it down under mini goals)

GOAL TYPE

○ Personal   ○ Health & Fitness   ○ Relationships

○ Financial   ○ Career   ○ Travel   ○ Lifetime

○ Other

MINI GOALS   (include up to 10 steps to achieve main goal)

☐

☐

☐

☐

☐

GOAL 74

☐

☐

☐

☐

☐

GOAL 75

Today's Date: **Target Date:**

Date Completed: **Goal Accomplished:** ☐

GOAL (describe your ultimate goal and then break it down under mini goals)

GOAL TYPE

○ Personal ○ Health & Fitness ○ Relationships

○ Financial ○ Career ○ Travel ○ Lifetime

○ Other

MINI GOALS (include up to 10 steps to achieve main goal)

☐

☐

☐

☐

☐

GOAL 75

☐

☐

☐

☐

☐

NOTES

GOAL 76

Today's Date: _____

Target Date: _____

Date Completed: _____

Goal Accomplished: ☐

GOAL (describe your ultimate goal and then break it down under mini goals)

GOAL TYPE

○ Personal   ○ Health & Fitness   ○ Relationships

○ Financial   ○ Career   ○ Travel   ○ Lifetime

○ Other

MINI GOALS (include up to 10 steps to achieve main goal)

☐

☐

☐

☐

☐

GOAL 76

- [ ]
- [ ]
- [ ]
- [ ]
- [ ]

NOTES

GOAL 77

Today's Date: _____   **Target Date:** _____

Date Completed: _____   **Goal Accomplished:** ☐

GOAL (describe your ultimate goal and then break it down under mini goals)

GOAL TYPE

○ Personal   ○ Health & Fitness   ○ Relationships

○ Financial   ○ Career   ○ Travel   ○ Lifetime

○ Other

MINI GOALS (include up to 10 steps to achieve main goal)

☐

☐

☐

☐

☐

GOAL 77

- [ ]
- [ ]
- [ ]
- [ ]
- [ ]

NOTES

GOAL 78

Today's Date: **Target Date:**

Date Completed: **Goal Accomplished:** ☐

GOAL (describe your ultimate goal and then break it down under mini goals)

GOAL TYPE

- ○ Personal
- ○ Health & Fitness
- ○ Relationships
- ○ Financial
- ○ Career
- ○ Travel
- ○ Lifetime
- ○ Other

MINI GOALS (include up to 10 steps to achieve main goal)

☐

☐

☐

☐

☐

GOAL 78

☐

☐

☐

☐

☐

GOAL 79

Today's Date: **Target Date:**

Date Completed: **Goal Accomplished:** ☐

GOAL   (describe your ultimate goal and then break it down under mini goals)

GOAL TYPE

- ○ Personal
- ○ Health & Fitness
- ○ Relationships
- ○ Financial
- ○ Career
- ○ Travel
- ○ Lifetime
- ○ Other

MINI GOALS   (include up to 10 steps to achieve main goal)

☐

☐

☐

☐

☐

GOAL 79

☐

☐

☐

☐

☐

GOAL 80

Today's Date: _____   **Target Date:** _____

Date Completed: _____   **Goal Accomplished:** ☐

GOAL (describe your ultimate goal and then break it down under mini goals)

GOAL TYPE

○ Personal   ○ Health & Fitness   ○ Relationships

○ Financial   ○ Career   ○ Travel   ○ Lifetime

○ Other

MINI GOALS (include up to 10 steps to achieve main goal)

☐

☐

☐

☐

☐

GOAL 80

☐

☐

☐

☐

☐

NOTES

GOAL 81

Today's Date: **Target Date:**

Date Completed: **Goal Accomplished:** ☐

GOAL
(describe your ultimate goal and then break it down under mini goals)

GOAL TYPE

○ Personal   ○ Health & Fitness   ○ Relationships

○ Financial   ○ Career   ○ Travel   ○ Lifetime

○ Other

MINI GOALS
(include up to 10 steps to achieve main goal)

☐

☐

☐

☐

☐

GOAL 81

☐

☐

☐

☐

☐

NOTES

GOAL 82

Today's Date: **Target Date:**

Date Completed: **Goal Accomplished:** ☐

GOAL (describe your ultimate goal and then break it down under mini goals)

GOAL TYPE

- ○ Personal
- ○ Health & Fitness
- ○ Relationships
- ○ Financial
- ○ Career
- ○ Travel
- ○ Lifetime
- ○ Other

MINI GOALS (include up to 10 steps to achieve main goal)

- ☐
- ☐
- ☐
- ☐
- ☐

GOAL 82

☐

☐

☐

☐

☐

NOTES

GOAL 83

Today's Date: **Target Date:**

Date Completed: **Goal Accomplished:** ☐

GOAL (describe your ultimate goal and then break it down under mini goals)

GOAL TYPE

- ○ Personal
- ○ Health & Fitness
- ○ Relationships
- ○ Financial
- ○ Career
- ○ Travel
- ○ Lifetime
- ○ Other

MINI GOALS (include up to 10 steps to achieve main goal)

☐

☐

☐

☐

☐

GOAL 83

☐

☐

☐

☐

☐

NOTES

GOAL 84

Today's Date: _____   **Target Date:** _____

Date Completed: _____   **Goal Accomplished:** ☐

GOAL	(describe your ultimate goal and then break it down under mini goals)

GOAL TYPE			
◯ Personal	◯ Health & Fitness	◯ Relationships
◯ Financial	◯ Career	◯ Travel	◯ Lifetime
◯ Other			

MINI GOALS (include up to 10 steps to achieve main goal)

- ☐
- ☐
- ☐
- ☐
- ☐

GOAL 84

- [ ]
- [ ]
- [ ]
- [ ]
- [ ]

GOAL 85

Today's Date: _____   **Target Date:** _____

Date Completed: _____   **Goal Accomplished:** ☐

GOAL (describe your ultimate goal and then break it down under mini goals)

GOAL TYPE

○ Personal   ○ Health & Fitness   ○ Relationships

○ Financial   ○ Career   ○ Travel   ○ Lifetime

○ Other

MINI GOALS (include up to 10 steps to achieve main goal)

☐

☐

☐

☐

☐

GOAL 85

- [ ]
- [ ]
- [ ]
- [ ]
- [ ]

NOTES

GOAL 86

Today's Date: **Target Date:**

Date Completed: **Goal Accomplished:** ☐

GOAL (describe your ultimate goal and then break it down under mini goals)

GOAL TYPE

- ◯ Personal
- ◯ Health & Fitness
- ◯ Relationships
- ◯ Financial
- ◯ Career
- ◯ Travel
- ◯ Lifetime
- ◯ Other

MINI GOALS (include up to 10 steps to achieve main goal)

- ☐
- ☐
- ☐
- ☐
- ☐

GOAL 86

☐

☐

☐

☐

☐

NOTES

GOAL 87

Today's Date: **Target Date:**

Date Completed: **Goal Accomplished:** ☐

| GOAL | (describe your ultimate goal and then break it down under mini goals) |

GOAL TYPE	○ Personal	○ Health & Fitness	○ Relationships
○ Financial	○ Career	○ Travel	○ Lifetime
○ Other			

| MINI GOALS | (include up to 10 steps to achieve main goal) |

☐

☐

☐

☐

☐

GOAL 87

☐

☐

☐

☐

☐

GOAL 88

Today's Date: Target Date:

Date Completed: Goal Accomplished: ☐

GOAL (describe your ultimate goal and then break it down under mini goals)

GOAL TYPE

- ◯ Personal
- ◯ Health & Fitness
- ◯ Relationships
- ◯ Financial
- ◯ Career
- ◯ Travel
- ◯ Lifetime
- ◯ Other

MINI GOALS (include up to 10 steps to achieve main goal)

- ☐
- ☐
- ☐
- ☐
- ☐

GOAL 88

- [ ]
- [ ]
- [ ]
- [ ]
- [ ]

NOTES

GOAL 89

Today's Date: **Target Date:**

Date Completed: **Goal Accomplished:** ☐

GOAL (describe your ultimate goal and then break it down under mini goals)

GOAL TYPE

- ☐ Personal
- ☐ Health & Fitness
- ☐ Relationships
- ☐ Financial
- ☐ Career
- ☐ Travel
- ☐ Lifetime
- ☐ Other

MINI GOALS (include up to 10 steps to achieve main goal)

- ☐
- ☐
- ☐
- ☐
- ☐

GOAL 89

☐

☐

☐

☐

☐

NOTES

GOAL 90

Today's Date: **Target Date:**

Date Completed: **Goal Accomplished:** ☐

GOAL (describe your ultimate goal and then break it down under mini goals)

GOAL TYPE
- ○ Personal
- ○ Health & Fitness
- ○ Relationships
- ○ Financial
- ○ Career
- ○ Travel
- ○ Lifetime
- ○ Other

MINI GOALS (include up to 10 steps to achieve main goal)

☐

☐

☐

☐

☐

GOAL 90

☐

☐

☐

☐

☐

NOTES

GOAL 91

Today's Date: **Target Date:**

Date Completed: **Goal Accomplished:** ☐

GOAL   (describe your ultimate goal and then break it down under mini goals)

GOAL TYPE

◯ Personal   ◯ Health & Fitness   ◯ Relationships

◯ Financial   ◯ Career   ◯ Travel   ◯ Lifetime

◯ Other

MINI GOALS   (include up to 10 steps to achieve main goal)

☐

☐

☐

☐

☐

GOAL 91

☐

☐

☐

☐

☐

GOAL 92

Today's Date: **Target Date:**

Date Completed: **Goal Accomplished:** ☐

GOAL (describe your ultimate goal and then break it down under mini goals)

GOAL TYPE

- ○ Personal
- ○ Health & Fitness
- ○ Relationships
- ○ Financial
- ○ Career
- ○ Travel
- ○ Lifetime
- ○ Other

MINI GOALS (include up to 10 steps to achieve main goal)

☐

☐

☐

☐

☐

GOAL 92

☐

☐

☐

☐

☐

NOTES

GOAL 93

Today's Date: **Target Date:**

Date Completed: **Goal Accomplished:** ☐

GOAL (describe your ultimate goal and then break it down under mini goals)

GOAL TYPE

- ○ Personal
- ○ Health & Fitness
- ○ Relationships
- ○ Financial
- ○ Career
- ○ Travel
- ○ Lifetime
- ○ Other

MINI GOALS (include up to 10 steps to achieve main goal)

- ☐
- ☐
- ☐
- ☐
- ☐

GOAL 93

☐

☐

☐

☐

☐

GOAL 94

Today's Date: **Target Date:**

Date Completed: **Goal Accomplished:** ☐

GOAL (describe your ultimate goal and then break it down under mini goals)

GOAL TYPE

- ○ Personal
- ○ Health & Fitness
- ○ Relationships
- ○ Financial
- ○ Career
- ○ Travel
- ○ Lifetime
- ○ Other

MINI GOALS (include up to 10 steps to achieve main goal)

☐

☐

☐

☐

☐

GOAL 94

☐

☐

☐

☐

☐

GOAL 95

Today's Date: **Target Date:**

Date Completed: **Goal Accomplished:** ☐

GOAL (describe your ultimate goal and then break it down under mini goals)

GOAL TYPE

○ Personal   ○ Health & Fitness   ○ Relationships

○ Financial   ○ Career   ○ Travel   ○ Lifetime

○ Other

MINI GOALS (include up to 10 steps to achieve main goal)

☐

☐

☐

☐

☐

GOAL 95

☐

☐

☐

☐

☐

NOTES

GOAL 96

Today's Date: _____   **Target Date:** _____

Date Completed: _____   **Goal Accomplished:** ☐

GOAL	(describe your ultimate goal and then break it down under mini goals)

GOAL TYPE	○ Personal	○ Health & Fitness	○ Relationships
○ Financial	○ Career	○ Travel	○ Lifetime
○ Other			

MINI GOALS	(include up to 10 steps to achieve main goal)

☐

☐

☐

☐

☐

GOAL 96

☐

☐

☐

☐

☐

GOAL 97

Today's Date: **Target Date:**

Date Completed: **Goal Accomplished:** ☐

GOAL   (describe your ultimate goal and then break it down under mini goals)

GOAL TYPE

○ Personal   ○ Health & Fitness   ○ Relationships

○ Financial   ○ Career   ○ Travel   ○ Lifetime

○ Other

MINI GOALS   (include up to 10 steps to achieve main goal)

☐

☐

☐

☐

☐

GOAL 97

☐

☐

☐

☐

☐

GOAL 98

Today's Date: **Target Date:**

Date Completed: **Goal Accomplished:** ☐

GOAL   (describe your ultimate goal and then break it down under mini goals)

GOAL TYPE

- ○ Personal
- ○ Health & Fitness
- ○ Relationships
- ○ Financial
- ○ Career
- ○ Travel
- ○ Lifetime
- ○ Other

MINI GOALS   (include up to 10 steps to achieve main goal)

☐

☐

☐

☐

☐

GOAL 98

☐

☐

☐

☐

☐

NOTES

GOAL 99

Today's Date: **Target Date:**

Date Completed: **Goal Accomplished:** ☐

GOAL (describe your ultimate goal and then break it down under mini goals)

GOAL TYPE

- ○ Personal
- ○ Health & Fitness
- ○ Relationships
- ○ Financial
- ○ Career
- ○ Travel
- ○ Lifetime
- ○ Other

MINI GOALS (include up to 10 steps to achieve main goal)

☐

☐

☐

☐

☐

GOAL 99

- [ ]
- [ ]
- [ ]
- [ ]
- [ ]

GOAL 100

Today's Date: ⬚⬚⬚⬚⬚ **Target Date:** ⬚⬚⬚⬚⬚

Date Completed: ⬚⬚⬚⬚⬚ **Goal Accomplished:** ☐

GOAL (describe your ultimate goal and then break it down under mini goals)

GOAL TYPE

- ○ Personal
- ○ Health & Fitness
- ○ Relationships
- ○ Financial
- ○ Career
- ○ Travel
- ○ Lifetime
- ○ Other

MINI GOALS (include up to 10 steps to achieve main goal)

- ☐
- ☐
- ☐
- ☐
- ☐

GOAL 100

☐

☐

☐

☐

☐

NOTES

NOTES

NOTES

NOTES

NOTES

NOTES

47490940R00120

Made in the USA
San Bernardino, CA
31 March 2017